ABC's for Grown-Ups

Lessons from Three-Year Olds on How to Have More Fun & Success

by

Veronica Lim

Inner Thinking UK Limited

Dedicated to my best friend, Jeff,
whose sense of fun rubs off on and
inspires everyone he meets

Inner Thinking UK Limited
3 Charleville Mansions
Charleville Road
London W14 9JB
www.innerthinking.com

Published by Inner Thinking UK Limited 2003

British Library Cataloging in Publication data available

ISBN 0 9545974 2 7

Printed in the UK

Setting a good example for children takes
all the fun out of middle age.

William Feather (1908 - 1976)

~ ~ ~ ~ ~

Children have neither a past nor a future.
Thus they enjoy the present - which seldom
happens to us.

Jean De La Bruyere (1645 - 1696)

ABC's
for Grown-Ups

Contents

A B C D E
Hello & Welcome!

Hello!

Remember back to your last vacation.... No, not the first few days, but the days near to the end. When you were truly relaxed. Remember?

How did you feel? I'm guessing that you were enthused, energetic, creative, fulfilled, happy, patient, smiling, giving, loving, fun-filled, appreciative, self-aware, content, free with yourself, peaceful..... and maybe dreading going home a little?

Now imagine what your normal life would be like if you could take those feelings back from vacation with you. Imagine if everyday was like that!

How much more effective yet relaxed would you be in your daily life? How much more would you be able to get out of your teams at work because you were behaving differently? How much more would you be enjoying yourself?

Have you noticed how carefree little children are? If you get the chance, watch a three-year old for a few hours and you'll see how in love with life they are. They are buzzing with energy! The world is their playground and they are here to simply have a good time, being themselves.

As adults, we have forgotten what that's like. Some of us feel trapped by responsibility. Sometimes we feel that we must think and do certain things because that's what others say we should. We play various roles according to whom we think we ought to be.

We've forgotten how to be ourselves, and we've forgotten how to really enjoy life as a playground of fun and experience. I think that we somehow got that way whilst we were growing up!

Being like a kid again gives you energy. You remember how to have fun, to laugh with delight, you relax and you remember how to be creative. You also learn to let go of much self-consciousness.

Imagine how life would be if you were totally carefree again. Imagine how you would be if those things that stress you out now just aren't so important anymore. Imagine waking up in the morning, raring to go, full of anticipation and wonder as to what the day will hold for you. Imagine believing in your dreams again. Imagine each day being a new adventure....

We would all benefit hugely from living our lives as children do - as a playground of experience. Life is a playground! Let's lighten up! Laugh at ourselves and enjoy each day as it comes. We can do it. We all can. We just have to remember how, and perhaps to give ourselves the permission to do so.

So how about learning your ABC's again? Practice an alphabet a fortnight, and I promise you, at the end of one year, your life will be transformed.

Veronica Lim
London, 2003

ABC's
for Grown-Ups

A-S-K to G-E-T

Somehow somewhere along the line, we learned how to not ask for what we want and need. Sometimes we want help, but we don't ask. Sometimes we actually NEED help, and still we don't ask!

Maybe we're too shy. Or maybe we feel ashamed to ask. It actually takes personal strength and confidence to ask for help.

Sometimes we expect the other person to be able to read our minds and know that we need help!

Why?! We can't mind-read! Even Lone Ranger had a partner! (Tonto, in case you can't remember).

Kids, on the other hand, are always asking for help.....when they can't open the door, when they don't know how to read a new or difficult word, when they can't reach for something, when they want help to visit the toilet. The list is endless.

And have you noticed that when they ask for help, no one minds giving them a hand? In fact, most people take pleasure in helping.

This is true of helping other people too, not just kids. Remember when someone asked you for your help? Didn't you feel secretly pleased that they had asked YOU and that you could help them?

So what stops you from asking for what you want and need?

After all, if you don't ask, you don't get. Remember, you have to A-S-K in order to G-E-T.

Action:
The next time you want something and you hesitate to ask, catch yourself. Remind yourself that you are offering the other

person the pleasure of helping another person. Remember also that they cannot mind-read. Then go ahead and make your request. And what if they say no? Well, you're no worse off than before, and you just opened up the possibility of their saying yes!

To Girls and Boys alike we say:
"Keep Bright Your Eyes for Work and Play!"
Read with a clear, good light falling from above over your shoulder.
Hold your book about fourteen inches from your eyes.
Always read with your head up.
Keep your books clean; a soiled page is hard to read.
Avoid books printed indistinctly, in small type, or on glossy paper.
Rest your eyes frequently.
If your eyes ache, or if you have any difficulty in seeing things distinctly, have your eyes examined.
RECOMMENDED BY
THE NATIONAL COMMITTEE FOR THE PREVENTION OF BLINDNESS

Bedtime stories

Children have a pre-bedtime routine. Often, it involves Mummy or Daddy tucking them into bed and reading them a bedtime story. Fully relaxed they drift off to sleep.

How about you? Do you have a pre-bedtime routine that allows you to relax gradually and surely, and then drift off to sleep?

Do you do some bedtime reading for half an hour before you turn out the lights? Or do you flop into bed after having been glued to the TV set for the entire evening?

Reading is a great way to get a daily dose of inspiration. There is so much to read and be inspired by! Take advantage of it.

In any case, do you have a pre-bedtime routine?

Action:

What can you do to allow yourself to wind down and relax fully before you turn out the lights? Oh and one other thing, it's also a great idea to go to bed on the same day that you woke up!

Curiosity Abounds

When you were a kid, did you drive someone crazy by your constant questioning? "Why?" "Yes, but why?"

Perhaps you've been driven up the walls yourself with some kid asking you the question, "Why?"

Children are curious. They are inquisitive. They always want to know. They want to know how, they want to know why, they want to know when, they want to know who, they want to know what, they want to know just about everything!

They have their noses in every nook and cranny, they are constantly exploring. I remember hearing my Mum telling the story of my brother sucking on baby snails, to check them out to see if they were like sweets. Children always want to know what something tastes like too!

They are always willing to experiment.

Watch a child with a large piece jigsaw puzzle. At first they can't get the piece into its slot. But they twist and turn the piece, trying different ways of slotting it in until they discover the solution.

When you're curious and when you're willing to experiment, you learn. You expand your thinking, you come up with new ideas. You keep going until your curiosity is satisfied. That's how some of the best inventions and latest innovations are born.

Action:
Expand your life experience. Challenge what is. Ask why. When was the last time you asked why you were doing something? Or why you were doing something a certain way. Ask, "What would happen if......" Ask, "How could I change this to make it better?" Be willing to experiment. See what comes up.

Notes

Dollops of fun

Can you recall the last time you had fun? I mean really had fun.

Dollops of fun.... where you laughed until your belly ached, you screamed with sheer delight and you grinned from ear to ear with the sheer joy of the experience?

Kids do it all the time! Watch them on a swing – "Higher, higher, push me higher!" Hear their screams and giggles of delight when they're being chased "by the monster". Feel their excitement as they take themselves to the next level, wanting to experience more, more, more, just to repeat that experience yet again. "Please. Just once more! Once more on the swing, pleeeaaaase!"

We are more creative and productive when we are having fun. We are much more pleasurable to live with, to work with and to get on with.

Other people are more open to helping people who are cheerful than those who are not. Plus people who work in a fun environment are more productive, and happy staff make for happy customers make for happy profits.

What better way to create a memory than through having fun?

Don't wait until your vacation or the weekend before you allow yourself to have fun. Do it now! At work, at home, with your friends, your colleagues, your family, your dog, your cat….

Action:
Think about all the times that you've had fun in the past. Make a list of the things you did, including those activities you enjoyed when you were a kid. Write down even those activities which you haven't done in a while. For example, going on a swing, playing a harmless practical joke on

someone. What else would make you smile? Do one fun activity every day. Relax and enjoy.

Eager Expectations

"It's coming up to Christmas! Write a letter to Santa Claus and ask for what you want!" And so children do.

Then they let it go, and they simply wait in eager anticipation. Their expectation is that what they asked for will show up. When Christmas arrives, it will be there.

Like the gardener who plants the seeds he or she puts into the soil, he waters them and nurtures them. Then he waits. Until one day, the young shoot appears. With further care and attention, the young plant develops and turns into a tree. Years later, it bears fruit – a rewarding crop for the years of care and attention.

In the fall, the leaves are shed and in the spring, new shoots and buds grow. Such is the cycle and rhythm of life. And in the meantime, the gardener never ceases giving the tree due care and attention. Never once does the gardener expect anything other than that. The expectation is always that the tree will bear its crop.

Yet when it comes to our own ideas and our dreams, the expectation can be different! Patient though eager anticipation gets lost as we constantly wonder why the results haven't showed up yet. Like the planted seed, our ideas need time to germinate, take root, then to grow and finally to bear fruit. And all the time, it needs focus and attention.

Be patient. From young acorns do oak trees grow.

Action:
Remember the seasons and be a gardener. Always expecting results, always anticipating results. Never wondering when the fruits are going to show. Trusting that the fruit will always happen. Be patient, and grow many trees.

Falling Down

I think it was Confucius who said, "Failure is not in falling down; failure is in failing to get up again."

There is no such thing as failure – only results. We are continually creating results in our lives. It just so happens that sometimes we are successful at creating a result that we don't want.

But, remember, many of our best lessons come from those occasions when we didn't do things "right".

When Thomas Edison "failed" at producing a working light bulb, he said, "I have not failed. I've just found 10,000 ways that won't work."

Unlike Edison, instead of focusing on the bright side of something not being quite right, many of us focus completely on what isn't right. Notice how we do that a lot of the time, and especially at work?

Then we replay the story over and over and over again. And we continue to beat ourselves up about it, over and over and over again.

Hey! If there was a song that you didn't like on your CD, would you keep on playing it over and over and over again?

Children may cry and fuss from the pain of having fallen down, but they always get up again. A few minutes later, they're off!

Pain all gone, the fall forgotten. Left behind and in the past.

We must all learn to do the same.

Action:
When things don't work out quite how you planned, look for what went well and what could make it even better for the next time

around. Focus on the positive lessons and acknowledge yourself for what went well. Then move on.

Gifts and Talents

Children love doing what they are naturally good at. They are often encouraged to carry on doing what they are good at and naturally love.

Until they get to school, that is. Then they start getting told other things, like "You must be good at all your subjects in school so that you can get a good job when you grow up." And the focus changes. Instead of getting praise and encouragement, suddenly the missing pieces are pointed out.

"Your Arithmetic was OK – you scored 95% in that. But your History – you only got 60%. You're going to have to study harder at History!"

So we end up forgetting that we had natural strengths, gifts and talents and we start noticing our weaknesses. With a vengeance!

We focus on these weaknesses, beat ourselves up over it, and then look for ways in which we can convert them into strengths. We think that by making ourselves do these things that we aren't naturally good at and generally don't like, it will make us miraculously good at it!

Hmmm.... We might get better at them and maybe we might even begin to enjoy them....

But what about harnessing our natural strengths instead and playing to those? We will get better and better at those things we are good at, we would enjoy it that much more and it would be effortless. We'd just have to be ourselves!

What could possibly be wrong with that?!

Action:
What are you naturally good at? What did you enjoy doing when you were a child? How do you use your strengths today? How do

you encourage the people who work with you to harness their natural strengths?

Hug a friend

Children love to be hugged, cuddled, kissed, tucked into bed, have their hair brushed, patted on the back and generally fussed over.

We don't lose that yearning as we grow up, but many of us do forget how good it is to be hugged, cuddled, have our hair brushed, patted on the back and generally fussed over. Or we get embarrassed – too unable to receive.

Touch is therapeutic. That is why massages are healing, relaxing and invigorating at the same time.

As human beings, we all need an element of touch, to feel loved, and to feel that we belong.

Give someone a hug to. . .

. . . celebrate

. . . say hello
. . . tell them you're their friend
. . . say well done!
. . . because it feels good

Action:
Give a friend or a family member a warm hug. Or your pet! Just remember how it feels to be hugged.

Notes

We dream...

Imagining & Dreaming

Children are always using their imagination and playing make-believe. When you were a child, did you have an imaginary friend? When you were a child playing Cowboys and Indians, you WERE that cowboy or Indian!

For kids, clouds in the sky can take on meaningful shapes, they can be a doctor one moment and a teacher the next, and then they are the brave pilot of the skies. Their trusted bicycle becomes a horse, and then anything that they want, now or in the future.

Everything can, and always will be, simply because they think it so. And they believe it to be so.

Then we get older, and we get told that daydreaming and imagining is bad for us. So we stop, and in the process, we also stop believing.

The truth is every greatest invention and every greatest business idea started first in someone's imagination.

Others may have thought it was a waste of time. But ask Fred Smith, the founder of Fed-Ex! His Yale Business School lecturer thought that Smith's idea would never work! Then ask Ted Turner, founder of Cable News Network (CNN). Everyone else thought that a 24 hour news cable channel would never work too!

Plus, have you heard of the power of "acting as if"? Acting as if you already are who you want to be actually helps to get you there more quickly and easily. But, you have to do it with total and congruent feeling and self-belief.

Action:
Start using your imagination again. Start day-dreaming about what you want. Create a picture of how you want things to be in your life, at work and at home. Add in the

smells, the sounds and the feelings too. Learn how to dream again. See yourself having accomplished whatever you aspire to. Got a problem? Imagine that you have solved it. Then think back from that position as to how you actually solved it. It's much easier.

Just for Fun

Do you sometimes find yourself saying, "Oh, I'm not creative" or "I'm not artistic"?

Codswallop. B.S.

Every single person is. That's our natural state. Only some of us have forgotten how. It's that growing up thing we do, again.

Children just get on with it. They don't stop to ask themselves whether they are artistic or creative; they just are. They just play the part of being creative. From building sand castles to painting masterpieces that most other people can't understand but yet can understand the beauty of.

And anyway, who says that creative means it's got to be beautiful or recognizable? Hey, beauty is in the eye of the beholder, and creativity is just for fun. Ask any kid.

Action:

Why stop to wonder or question whether you are or are not? Does it really matter as long as it gives you joy? Simply allow yourself to be, for the sheer enjoyment of self-expression. Who cares?

Know What You Want

Children just know what they want. They can be oh-so-focused on it much to the frustration of their parents at times!

They are clear about what they want. I want to be fed...I want that toy....I want to stay up late....I want to be read a story. They even know exactly which story they want read to them. (And they know when you try and skip a page whilst they aren't looking! They know it's not the whole enchilada and they make you go back to the bit you missed!)

As adults, most of us know what we don't want. That's easy. I don't want to work here anymore. I don't want to have such a high level of stress. I don't want to do this. I don't want to live here.

Yet many of us don't know what we really want. That's rather more difficult!

Try it out and see. Next time someone complains about something, stop them and ask them what they want instead.

Think about it. If you don't know what you want, how can you get it? You can't get what you want until you know what it is that you want.

Action:
Start by making a list of all the things you don't want – in your work, your relationship, your finances, etc. Use that as a starting point for your list of what you do want, and then keep adding to it. Now, pick out the top three items which you feel most inspired to turn into reality and just do it!

Living in the Present

Children are totally focused on the present moment. They concentrate fully on what's in front of them. They don't worry about yesterday or feel anxious about what's going to happen tomorrow. They enjoy the gift of the present.

Have you noticed that children are more "observant" than adults as a whole? The little child will notice the bird in the tree, whilst most adults just pass it by. The child will notice the flower on the sidewalk, whilst most adults are lost in their thoughts.

We cannot re-live the past, except in our thoughts. We cannot live in the future, except in our thoughts. Yet we often create regret and anxiety by thinking about the past or the future.

The only time that we live and experience is in the present moment, the here and now.

So learn from the past, plan for the future and live each present moment to the very fullest. It's gone in an instant.

Action:

Take time to notice. Notice the colors, the smells, the sounds, what you see and what you feel.... in each particular moment. Be mindfully aware of your surroundings, and take it all in. Stop thinking those thoughts that keep on going around in your head – at least for a moment or two. Living is now.

Notes

Magic

Watch the wonder in a child's face when they think about Santa Claus. Watch the wonder in a child's face when they see a magic trick for the first time.

If we aren't open to magic, we will never recognize the magic in our lives. It doesn't take a miracle for something to be magic. It doesn't have to be enormous to be magic.

Magic can be found in the simplest things.

....a smile
....the sunshine after the rain
....a rainbow
....a sunny spring day
....golden leaves in the fall
....a traffic jam, for slowing you down enough to notice the green fields
....catching up with old friends
....the stars in the sky
....the moon at night
....the touch of your partner's hand

....a team to work with at work
....a bird on the windowsill....

Action:
Look for the magic in everything. Look for the magic in the smallest of things. Create magic in all that you say and do, purely for your own pleasure of knowing that you can. Go on and create... your very own magic.

Now, Listen to Me!

Kids! They always insist on being heard! They will assert themselves into a conversation, speaking more and more loudly and insistently, asserting themselves more and more, until they have gained the full attention they desire.

OK, sometimes they interrupt. You don't need to do that, but you can make sure that you get heard.

It's your responsibility to get heard. Not theirs. You owe it to yourself.

Action:
Each day, be assertive in one small situation. Start with small steps......

Oh My Belly Aches!

Listen to a baby gurgle. Listen to a child laugh with glee. Hear someone laugh, a deep belly laugh. And feel how infectious it is.

Laughter heals. Laughter lightens. Laughter is good for the heart. Laughter is good for the soul. Laughter is good for feeling good!

Laugh.... Until your belly aches!

Action:
Laugh out loud. Read a joke a day. Tell a joke a day. Find the funny side. Appreciate the gift of laughter. Take joy in things.

Notes

Presents for Me!

Offer a child a gift and watch.

Children put out their hand, eager to receive the present that they are being offered. They thrill at the thought of receiving a present and they thrive in any praise that they receive.

Somewhere along the way, we unlearn how to receive. When someone pays us a compliment, we may dismiss it with the thought, "They are just saying that". Or we counter it with, "Does that mean that I look bad on other days?"

Why not simply and graciously accept the gift or compliment with a smile, a thank you and a silent acknowledgement for yourself? Share the joy of receiving with the person who is giving. Allow them the joy of giving with a gracious and grateful "Thank you".

Action:

Start practicing by giving yourself compliments. No qualifications. Just compliments. Pure and simple, and unadulterated. (Ooh, big word.... And notice... it's un-ADULT-erated!)

Question Time

Children observe all the time, they listen and they learn. They ask questions.

When we've learnt and we think we know it all, we close ourselves off to further learning. We fail to spot the new aspect, the new lesson, the freshness of something new. We fail to listen and observe with an open mind. We jump to conclusions. We don't stop to listen actively to what the other person is saying until they have finished saying what they have to say. We get too busy thinking up our response. We stop listening when we've thought of what we're going to say. We say, "I know that". We deprive ourselves of a new learning experience.

What were you saying?

Action:
When you come across something you feel you already know, catch yourself and stop

yourself from the familiar thoughts of, "I know this already". Think instead, "What else could I learn from this by staying open, observing and listening, as if I don't already know it?" Unsuccessful people say, "This doesn't fit in with what I think, I'm going to discard it." Successful people say, "Hmm, this doesn't fit in with what I know, but if I took it on board, how could it help me?" Which person would you most like to model?

75 North to 475 Get off at
1st exit - Hill Rd. turn left
(West) Go down pass Fenton Rd
on Left side Urological
G-1121 Across from
Services
Home Depot

pager 810-972-2200

Shannon's # 810-241-8329

Fenton South.

rt on Fenton Grand Blanc pass 2nd light
road Baldwin turn left - east
second drive on left (Timber Ridge turn
left (No) to pack Castle oak 9412 Bldg.
Behind porta potty.

Place the potatoes in a medium pot and cover with wate
about 15 minutes. Drain and when cool enough to handl
slices.

Peel stems of cardoons with a vegetable peeler. Discard
water with milk, until tender, about 3 minutes. Remove a

In a small bowl, combine thyme, garlic, red pepper flake

In a large oval casserole dish, alternately layer at an an
and zucchini, seasoning between each layer with garlic
the olive oil and bake until the vegetables are tender ar
Sprinkle the cheese over the top and return to the oven

Remove from the oven and serve hot.

Episode#: EM1F06

Notes

Run, Hop, Skip and Jump

When you don't have young children of your own, it can be tiring watching other people's children in action. They're constantly on the move. Up and down, round and round, into this and into that. Phew. I need a rest! Just where do they get the energy from?

Kids have an enthusiasm about everything they decide to do. Watch their animated faces. You know when they're bored – they turn their attention to something else.

What would it take for you to be fully engaged in what you are doing in each particular moment?

Purposefulness. Not hurry, but purposefulness.

Walk with purpose. Talk with purpose. Do your work with purpose. Relax with purpose. Even if your purpose is just pure fun.

In fact, make your primary purpose to have pure fun, to enjoy yourself. Yes, at work too – it's possible! And also to be recommended!

Then have a secondary purpose on top of that.

Take a leaf out of the kiddies' book too. Exercise – with purpose.

Action:
What are you currently doing out of sheer routine with no purpose or meaning? How can you inject more purpose and meaning into it? Oh, and fit in some exercise too. It's good for all mind, body and soul.

Selfishness? Yes!

"Don't be selfish," we're told. And what many people have taken that to mean is, "Put others first and leave yourself out of the picture completely."

Uh-oh. That's where we got it wrong. It's great to be selfish – healthily selfish, that is.

Being healthily selfish is to do something because, "selfishly", it makes YOU feel good. Really good. And because you feel soooo good, everyone else around you benefits too. See the difference?

To be healthily selfish is to do things for yourself so you feel good, and as a result you can't help but be a better person and to be there more for others.

You can't give away that which you do not have. So start with yourself.

Action:

Stop feeling guilty when you do something for yourself. Notice how being healthily selfish positively impacts on you and your relationships – both at home and at work. Discover what makes you feel good. And remember, there is nothing more important that that you feel good.

Thank You!

When we were little, our parents encouraged us and praised us constantly and consistently. When we said our first words, when we started to crawl, when we started to take our first steps, when we started to read....

We graciously accepted those encouraging words. In fact we lapped them up! And we looked for ways in which we could do more of the same, so that we could please our parents again and be praised and encouraged even more.

As adults, we often reject or belittle words of praise and encouragement. When someone says, "Hey, you did a really good job there", we say things like, "Oh, it was easy. Anyone could have done it." Or we think to ourselves, "They're only saying that, they don't really mean it." Or perhaps, "I'm just doing my job".

Are you guilty of this yourself?

The job may well have been easy (well, at least for you). Someone else may well be able to do it too. But having done a good job is having done a good job!

Accept it, old pal!

Action:
Smile, say thank you graciously. Let those words of praise and encouragement sink in. Acknowledge yourself for what you've done. Pat yourself on the back. Feel pleased with yourself. Then thank yourself and remind yourself to do it again.

Notes

Unconditional Friends

Children just seem able to swan off and make new friends with other children. They may start off being a little bit shy, and then they're checking out their new friends.... Oh to be playing with new pals!

Children don't pre-judge in the same way as many adults do. They unconditionally accept others just as they accept themselves. "That's just the way the other person is and this is just the way I am".

We grow up and our expectations change – of ourselves and of others too. We have expectations – on how to behave, what to say, what to not say, how to dress, where to go, what kind of job to have, what kind of car to drive. We judge others (and ourselves) on that. We judge by their job, their salary, their car.... Our job, our salary, our car....

Even worse, we often allow ourselves to get agitated by other people's behavior.

The bus driver was gruff when I asked for an incorrect ticket. I could have gotten angry. How rude he was! To me! I could have gotten agitated, and I would have had every right!

But hey, how do I know what might have happened for him that morning? Perhaps he had had a fight with his partner? What do I know? It's not personal.... And definitely not worth my getting upset and spoiling my day.... My choice.

Your choice.

Action:
Adopt the assumption that everybody does the best that they can and know how to, at that particular moment in time. No, it's not an excuse for them. It's a valid reason for you – so you don't get stressed out in the first place. (Isn't that a good enough reason

to adopt this assumption? Think of yourself first for a change!) Accept them for what and who they are.

Volunteer Me!

Children want to "be in" on everything. They want to "help", with the gardening, the cleaning, the shopping, the you-name-it. They want to help, to be involved. They volunteer, just for the enjoyment of the experience.

Then we grow up and learn on the way, to keep ourselves to ourselves. We may even refrain from volunteering for something that we would very much like to do. We can become afraid of "showing ourselves up".

We don't see that the elderly person with those heavy parcels could do with some help. We don't volunteer a smile or a friendly greeting to our fellow-travelers in the morning. We bury ourselves in our own internal thoughts. And when someone strikes up a conversation, we wish they would stop intruding on our privacy.

We rush around for feeling a lack of time, yet we lose track of time for getting lost in our own thoughts. But, have you ever noticed how the busiest of people always seem to have the time?

Action:
When you want to do something, get involved! Volunteer. Get stuck in. Offer your help, take action. Ahhhhh. Enjoy.

Wholehearted Self-expression

Have you seen a child in a temper? They really get into it – wholeheartedly. See how they scrunch up their faces, stamp their feet and hear the expression in their voices. They really make their feelings known.

Then catch them when they're excited about something. Eyes wide open, popping out of their heads. "Let's go! What are we waiting for?!"

Now you.

When was the last time that you fully acknowledged and expressed your own feelings? Or do you bury or deny them?

Years ago, I took three months off to travel the world. Wow, was I excited! And one day, someone asked me, "Aren't you excited?" to which I replied, "Of course! Can't you see I'm grinning from ear to ear?"

Hmmm.

Expressing your feelings doesn't necessarily mean screaming or shouting, but how about letting your self-restraint go a little and REALLY expressing those good feelings so you feel it all over?

Action:
Give yourself permission to be spontaneous. When you don't like something, say it, in a way that helps the other person understand. But say it. When you DO like something, say it, show it, feel it, taste it, hear it, share it, and everything-else-it that you can think of!

Xcellent Ideas

The next time you see young children having a discussion amongst themselves, just stop and watch for a moment. See how they come up with ideas....

Let's play "Cowboys & Indians!" "No, let's play Tomb-Raider!" "No, let's pretend to be firemen!" "OK, let's play Farmyard Animals"....

See how they come up with ideas about what goes where, how things can be, how things can be fixed. No hesitation about whether it can actually be done or not – everything is possible. Everything is a potentially excellent idea. Everything is worth mentioning. Everything is worth consideration.

The next time you need some excellent ideas, forget about possibility and forget about practicality. Get the ideas out into the open. Then when you have completely run out of ideas, look at each idea in turn.

But be careful! Don't make the mistake of trying to see what is wrong with that idea. Instead, see how it can be implemented. Then whittle the ideas down.

Finally and finally, let the analytical, critical types in to look at it from the perspective of what problems they might anticipate with your final selection of ideas. They'll ask you questions which will further stimulate ideas, and weed out the definite no's.

Action:
Don't clamp down on your ideas too soon. Let them surface and bubble up. Let them generate other more creative ideas. Let your mind run free with being innovative. Then and only then start to look at each idea more closely.

Yes! Yes! Yes!

Kids simply know how to say "no" when it suits them.

Have you seen a defiant child, saying no simply because they know they can? It doesn't mean that they get their own way, but they surely know how to say "no".

At other times, when they hear "no" back as an answer, they go into negotiation mode. "Come on now, it's bedtime." "No!" "I told you, it's bedtime, say goodnight." "Ohhh. Five more minutes?" they say. "No." "Three?"

Who often wins?

As adults, we often find it difficult to say no. We may be afraid of hurting the other person's feelings. Sometimes it may be because we don't know what we want in the first place! Or we may be concerned about other people not liking us anymore if we say no.

Every time you say yes to someone else when you really want to say no, you are denying yourself. You're really saying no to yourself.

Think about the longer term effect of continually saying no to yourself....

What's stopping you from saying yes to yourself by saying no to someone else when this is what you really want?

Yes, yes, yes, yes, yes, yes, yes!

Action:
Work out what is important to you. Put yourself first. Practice saying no, first of all to the little things, and then to the bigger things which don't fall in line with your priorities. If you find this a particular challenge for you, ask your friends and family for support; explain what you are doing and ask them to help you. You may even consider working with a coach to help you get there.

Zzzzzz........

Children re-energize and re-charge their batteries every day, in the middle of the day by having a nap.

When was the last time you did that?

OK, so you can't quite pull out a sofa-bed in the middle of your office and take a nap. But how about fifteen minutes of quiet time? Time for yourself. No phones, no people, no thinking, nothing. Nada.

Just total peace and quiet.

Just fifteen minutes.

Need another reason? OK, Thomas Edison, the inventor of the light bulb said, "When you become quiet, it just dawns on you". What better way to find the solutions you are looking for.

Action:
Do it now. Do it everyday. And definitely, take a snooze in the middle of the afternoon at the weekends.

C
B
A

Notes

Info on how to get more copies of ABC's

For information on using *ABC's for Grown-Ups* for bulk purchases, sales promotions and premiums, please contact the publisher at: Inner Thinking UK Limited, 3 Charleville Mansions, Charleville Road, London W14 9JB. Telephone: 07092 33 55 75

Be sure to visit our websites at:
www.innerthinking.com
www.millionairethinking.com

Also, please send your feedback and success stories to:
veronica@millionairethinking.com

Notes

About the Author

Veronica Lim is the founder of Millionaire Thinking® - Having a Ball Having it All - Creating Lifetime Wealth.

Veronica has worked with hundreds of individuals through her coaching and seminars. She teaches all her clients how to have a freer, easier and richer life. Her knowledge is highly valuable to anyone who wants to make a positive change in their personal or business situation and well-being. She has an ability to explain concepts in a way that makes it easy for her readers, clients and seminar participants to understand and apply.

A chartered accountant, MBA and graduate of both Coach University and Corporate Coach University International, Veronica is also a member of the International Coach Federation and a Master Practitioner of NLP (Neuro-Linguistic Programming), and Time Line Therapy™.

Originally from Malaysia, she now lives in London, UK. Veronica dedicates some of her time to the Appeals Committee for the Westminster Society for People with Learning Disabilities, and loves reading, learning, ski-ing and golf. But most of all, she just loves having fun.

Printed in the United States
1375100006B/127-147